God Bless you –

Love –

Great Grandma Bentley

Important Prayers

THE SIGN OF THE CROSS

In the name of the Father, and of the Son, and of the Holy Spirit. Amen.

GLORY BE

Glory to the Father and to the Son and to the Holy Spirit: as it was in the beginning, is now and will be for ever. Amen.

GRACE BEFORE MEALS

Bless us, O Lord, and these your gifts which we are about to receive from Your bounty, through Christ our Lord. Amen.

GRACE AFTER MEALS

We give you thanks, almighty God, for these and all your gifts which we have received through Christ our Lord. Amen.

THE OUR FATHER

Our Father, who art in heaven,
hallowed be thy name.
Thy kingdom come.
Thy will be done on earth,
as it is in heaven.
Give us this day our daily bread,
and forgive us our trespasses,
as we forgive those
who trespass against us,
and lead us not into temptation,
but deliver us from evil. Amen.

THE HAIL MARY

Hail Mary, full of grace,
the Lord is with you;
blessed are you among women,
and blessed is the fruit
of thy womb, Jesus.
Holy Mary, Mother of God,
pray for us sinners now
and at the hour of our death. Amen.

General Prayers

ACT OF FAITH

O my God, I believe that you are
one God in three Divine Persons:
Father, Son and Holy Spirit.
I believe that your Divine Son
became man and died for our sins,
and that he will come again to
judge the living and the dead.
I believe these and all the truths
that the Catholic Church teaches,
because you have revealed them,
who can neither deceive nor
be deceived. Amen.

ACT OF HOPE

O my God, relying on your almighty
power and infinite mercy
and promises, I hope to obtain
pardon of my sins, the help
of your grace and life everlasting
through the merits of Jesus Christ,
my Lord and Redeemer. Amen.

ACT OF LOVE

O my God, I love you above all things
with my whole heart and soul,
because you are all good
and worthy of all love.
I love my neighbor as myself
for the love of you.
I forgive all who have injured me
and ask pardon of all
whom I have injured. Amen.

THE APOSTLES' CREED

I believe in God, the Father almighty,
creator of heaven and earth.
I believe in Jesus Christ, his only Son,
our Lord. He was conceived
by the power of the Holy Spirit
and born of the Virgin Mary.
He suffered under Pontius Pilate,
was crucified, died, and was buried.
He descended to the dead.
On the third day he rose again.
He ascended into heaven,
and is seated at the right hand
of the Father.
He will come again
to judge the living and the dead.
I believe in the Holy Spirit,
the holy Catholic Church,
the communion of saints,
the forgiveness of sins,
the resurrection of the body,
and the life everlasting. Amen.

Morning and Evening Prayers

When you wake up in the morning, kneel down and make the Sign of the Cross. Say the Our Father, the Hail Mary, the Glory Be, and the Apostles' Creed.

A MORNING OFFERING

O Sacred Heart of Jesus,
I offer you this day
all my thoughts, words,
desires, and actions.
Help me do everything for you.

THE GUARDIAN ANGEL PRAYER

Angel of God, my guardian dear,
To whom His love commits me here,
Ever this day be at my side
To light and guard, to rule and guide.
Amen.

Acts of Faith, Hope and Love

God, I believe all the truths which you have taught us.

God, I hope for your grace on earth and for eternal life with you in heaven.

God, I love you with all my heart.

God, I am sorry for all my sins. Help me never to commit them any more.

O sweetest Heart of Jesus, I implore that I may ever love you more and more.

Mary, you are my loving mother. Keep me near you and your dear son, Jesus, today.

Saint Joseph, watch over me today just as you protected and cared for the Child Jesus.

Evening Prayers

Before you go to bed, kneel down and make the Sign of the Cross. Say the Our Father, the Hail Mary, and the Glory be.

I adore you, God, I belong entirely to you. I kneel in your presence and adore you, my Lord and my God.

I thank you, God for keeping me safe all day. Watch over me tonight. All that I have and all that I am, I have received from you.

I believe that you are here, God. I lay myself down to rest in your sight.

I hope, God, that you will protect me always, day and night, and will bring me safely through the years of this life to the life everlasting.

Prayers to Mary

THE MEMORARE

Remember,
O most gracious Virgin Mary,
that never was it known
that anyone who fled
to your protection,
implored your help or sought your
intercession was left unaided.
Inspired with this confidence,
I fly to you,
O Virgin of virgins, my Mother.
To you I come, before you I stand,
sinful and sorrowful.
O Mother of the Word Incarnate,
do not ignore my petitions,
but in your mercy
hear and answer me. Amen.

HAIL, HOLY QUEEN

Hail, holy Queen,
Mother of mercy!
Hail, our life,
our sweetness and hope!
To you do we cry,
poor banished children of Eve;
to you do we send up our sighs,
mourning and weeping
in this valley of tears!
Turn then, most gracious advocate,
your eyes of mercy toward us;
and after this, our exile,
show unto us the blessed
fruit of your womb, Jesus.
O clement, O loving,
O sweet Virgin Mary.

Prayers to Jesus

SOUL OF CHRIST

Soul of Christ, sanctify me.
Body of Christ, save me.
Blood of Christ, inebriate me.
Water from the side of Christ,
wash me.

Passion of Christ, strengthen me.
O good Jesus, hear me.
Within your wounds hide me.

Separated from you, let me never be.
From the malignant enemy, defend me.

At the hour of death, call me.
To come to you, bid me,
that I may praise you
in the company of your saints,
for all eternity. Amen.

The Rosary

THE JOYFUL MYSTERIES

1. The Annuniation
2. The Visitation
3. The Nativity
4. The Presentation
5. The Finding in the Temple

THE MYSTERIES OF LIGHT

1. The Baptism of Jesus
2. The Wedding at Cana
3. The Proclamation of the Kingdom of God
4. The Transfiguration
5. The Institution of the Holy Eucharist

THE SORROWFUL MYSTERIES

1. Jesus' Agony in the Garden
2. The Scourging at the Pillar
3. The Crowning with Thorns
4. Jesus Carries His Cross
5. The Crucifixion

THE GLORIOUS MYSTERIES

1. The Resurrection
2. The Ascension
3. The Descent of the Holy Spirit
4. The Assumption of Mary
5. The Crowning of Mary

Stations of the Cross

This is a prayer said during Lent. Many people say it all year round. There are fourteen stations.

Prayer:
Jesus, I want to be sorry for my sins.
Help me to see how you suffered
and died for me.
Help me to know your mercy
and forgiveness.
Teach me how to say "Thank You."

1. **JESUS IS CONDEMNED TO DIE**
   I am sorry, Jesus.

2. **JESUS CARRIES HIS CROSS**
   It looks so heavy, Jesus.

3. **JESUS FALLS FOR THE FIRST TIME**
   Your strength is starting to fail.

4. JESUS MEETS HIS MOTHER MARY
How sad your Mother felt, Jesus.

5. SIMON HELPS JESUS
I must help others who carry
heavy loads.

6. VERONICA WIPES JESUS' FACE
Teach me to help others in need.

7. JESUS FALLS A SECOND TIME
Dear Jesus, how weak you are.

8. JESUS MEETS THE WOMEN
Jesus you are so brave. You tell
them not to cry.

9. JESUS FALLS THE THIRD TIME
Dear Jesus, you are suffering
so much.

10. **Jesus is Stripped of His Clothes**
How shamefully you were treated.

11. **Jesus is nailed to the cross**
How cruel the people were.
I love you.

12. **Jesus Dies**
I know you forgive me my sins.

13. **Jesus is taken down**
I thank the people who took care
of your body.

14. **Jesus is laid in the tomb**
Thank you for your mercy.

Prayer Before a Crucifix

Look down upon me, good and gentle Jesus, while before your face I humbly kneel and with burning soul pray and beg you to fix deep in my heart lively feelings of faith, hope and charity, true contrition for my sins, and a firm purpose of amendment.

While I contemplate, with great love and tender pity, your five most precious wounds, pondering over them within me and calling to mind the words which David, your prophet, said of you, my Jesus:

"They have pierced my hands and my feet, they have numbered all my bones." Amen.

—— MY FIRST ——
Prayer Book

Written
Sr. Karen Cavanaugh

Illustrated by
William Luberoff

Regina
Press